ISAAC ASIMOV'S
Library of the Universe

Quasars, Pulsars, and Black Holes

by Isaac Asimov

Gareth Stevens
London • Milwaukee

A note from the editors: In the United States and other places — including this book — a billion is the number represented by 1 followed by nine zeroes —1,000,000,000. In other countries, including Britain, this number is often called 'a thousand million', and one billion would then be represented by *12* zeroes — 1,000,000,000,000: a million million, which is called a 'trillion' in this book.

A special thanks to Adolf Schaller.

The reproduction rights to all photographs and illustrations in this book are controlled by the individuals or institutions credited on page 32 and may not be reproduced without their permission.

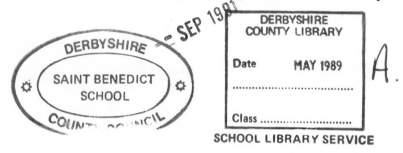
A Gareth Stevens Children's Books edition. Edited, designed, and produced by

Gareth Stevens, Inc.
7317 West Green Tree Road   Milwaukee, Wisconsin 53223, USA

ISBN 0-8368-7026-3
Text copyright © 1988 by Nightfall, Inc.
End matter copyright © 1988 by Gareth Stevens, Inc. and Martin Greenberg
Format copyright © 1988 by Gareth Stevens, Inc.

First published in the United States and Canada by Gareth Stevens, Inc.
First published in the United Kingdom in 1988 by Gareth Stevens Children's Books

Cover painting © Mark Paternostro

Designer: Laurie Shock
Picture research: Kathy Keller
Artwork commissioning: Kathy Keller and Laurie Shock
Project editors: Mark Sachner and Rhoda Irene Sherwood

Technical adviser and consulting editor: Greg Walz-Chojnacki

1 2 3 4 5 6 7 8 9 9 93 92 91 90 89 88

CONTENTS

Introduction

The Universe we live in is an enormously large place. Only in the last 50 years or so have we learned how large it really is. It's only natural that we would want to understand the place we live in, so in the last 50 years we have developed new instruments to help us learn about it. We have probes, satellites, radio telescopes, and many other things that tell us far more about the Universe than could possibly be imagined when I was young.

Nowadays, human beings have walked on the Moon. We have seen planets up close. We have mapped Venus through its clouds. We have seen dead volcanoes on Mars and live ones on Io, one of Jupiter's moons. We have learned amazing facts about how the Universe was born and have some ideas about how it may die. Nothing can be more astonishing and more interesting.

We have learned new things about the stars, too. Fifty years ago, the Universe seemed a quiet place. The stars seemed serene and unchanging. Now we know that stars can explode and leave behind bits of themselves that do amazing things. These bits are called neutron stars, or pulsars. We know that galaxies can have incredibly active centers, called quasars, and that there can be black holes in space. Everything can fall into them. Nothing can come out!

In this book, we will learn something about these fascinating things existing among the stars.

The Birth of Stars

The stars do not stay still. And they do not always behave themselves! Some twinkle, and some explode. Some collapse, and some collide with other stars. Some even swallow up light.

With its billions upon billions of stars, it is no wonder our Universe is such a wild place!

To begin with, the Universe was filled with large clouds of dust and gas. Some of these clouds began to contract under their own gravitational pull. In each of these clouds, the matter packed together and became hot. Finally, it became packed enough and hot enough to be a star. Our Sun formed this way nearly five billion years ago.

Stars still form out of clouds of dust and gas that exist today. One such cloud is the Orion Nebula, where astronomers can see small, dark, round spots. These are collapsing clouds that will eventually become shining stars.

The birth of the Sun. Upper left: The birth of the Sun began with the collapse of a cloud of gas and dust. Centre: As the cloud contracted, the outer regions flattened into a disk. Right: The centre erupted in a blaze — the Sun was born!

The Orion Nebula: A spectacular cloud of gases surrounds several hot stars deep inside the nebula. This cloud is visible to the naked eye as the middle star in the sword of the constellation Orion. See for yourself some night!

The Life of Stars

Stars come in all sizes. Some are larger and brighter than the Sun; some smaller and dimmer. They are all mostly hydrogen, which is the smallest element. Tiny particles of this hydrogen smash together into larger particles that make up helium, the next biggest element. This collision releases energy that keeps the stars shining. The energy also keeps them from collapsing under their own gravitational pull. Large stars have more hydrogen to begin with, but their centres are hotter than the centres of small stars. So large stars burn their hydrogen more quickly than small stars do.

The creation of helium. The illustration at right shows how the fusion of hydrogen into helium might be performed on Earth to create energy. The two atoms of hydrogen in the form of deuterium (upper left) and tritium (lower left) actually have a bit more mass than the helium (lower right) and neutron (upper right) that are made by this process. The difference in the mass is made up by a huge release of energy. A different form of fusion produces helium in the Sun — and creates sunshine.

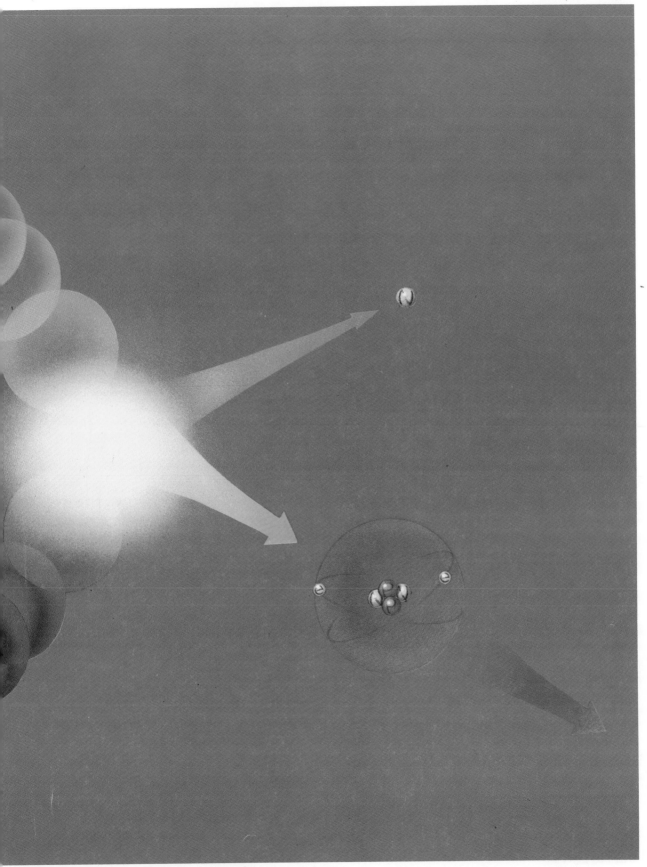

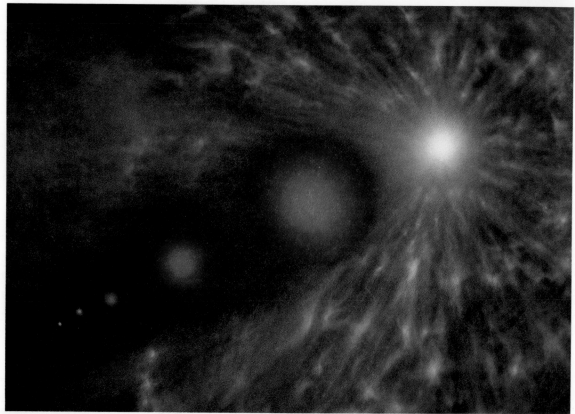

From star to supernova: Going out in style!

A Star's Violent End — From Red Giant to Supernova

As a star continues to shine, its centre grows steadily hotter, and its hydrogen runs low. The extra heat makes it expand. Because of this expansion, the outer layers change to a cool red. The result is a red giant. As the red giant continues to shine, it finally runs out of energy at the centre. Then it collapses.

This collapse heats the cool, red, outer layers, and, if the star is a big one, these layers explode. This large, exploding star becomes a supernova. For a while, the explosion makes it shine as brightly in the sky as a whole galaxy ordinarily does.

After such an explosion, matter flies into space or remains behind. The matter that remains behind will become a neutron star or a black hole.

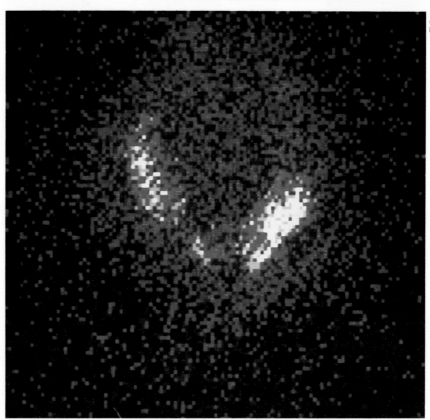

Supernova remnant: This is a satellite's computerized
image of material blasted out by an exploding star,
or supernova.

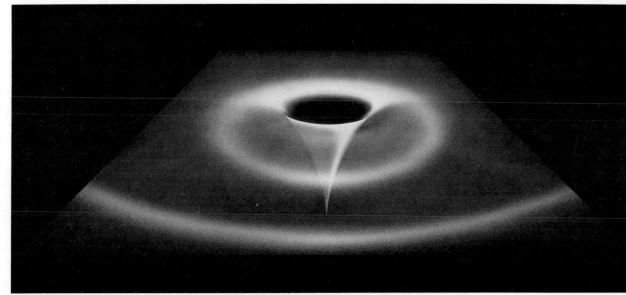

Black hole: What remains of a star after it explodes can be so dense
that it may imprison even its own light. Though it may be called a hole,
it is really an object of great mass. This illustration shows how the
immense gravity of the dead star creates a deep 'well' from which
nothing can escape.

The Big Squeeze
— A White Dwarf

When an ordinary star like the Sun collapses, its gravity squeezes it down to the size of a small planet. All the mass is there, but it has become a small, white-hot body called a white dwarf. If the mass of the Sun were squeezed into an object the size of Earth, or less, a bit of the white-dwarf matter about the size of your little finger would weigh at least 18 tonnes (20 tons). If the star is larger than the Sun to begin with, its greater gravity forces it together even more tightly. It becomes a neutron star, with all the mass of an ordinary star squeezed into a little ball perhaps 16 km (10 miles) across!

How much is 18 tonnes (20 tons)? This picture gives you an idea. It also gives you an idea of what happens when a star collapses into a white dwarf or a neutron star. Imagine an 18-tonne (20- ton) cement mixer collapsing into a white dwarf cement mixer the size of your little finger and still weighing 18 tonnes (20 tons)!

William Priedhorsky

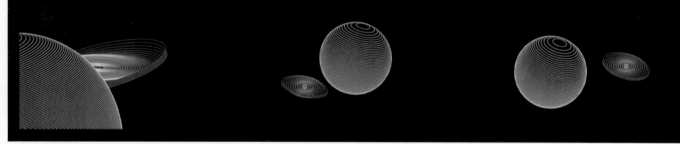

These pictures show a double star system. The larger star (yellow) is a normal star. Its smaller companion is a neutron star. Around the neutron star is an accretion disk. The disk is made up of matter from the normal star that has been sucked away by the neutron star's intense gravity. This matter forms the swirling accretion disk and hits the surface of

© Lynette Cook 1988

A neutron star – small matter, lots of mass!

Our Sun is too small to collapse into a neutron star. But what if a star the size of our Sun <u>could</u> collapse into a neutron star? All its mass would be squeezed into a ball only eight miles (13 km) across. The neutron star would take up only one-quadrillionth of the space the Sun would. But a piece of its matter would weigh a quadrillion (1,000,000,000,000,000) times more than the same size piece of matter from the Sun. Suppose you made a ball-point pen out of neutron star matter. A pen of ordinary matter might weigh half an ounce (14 grams). But a pen of neutron star matter would weigh 15 billion tons.

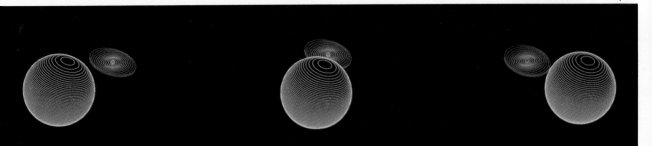

the neutron star at the centre of the disk. The neutron star's gravity is so great that when matter hits the neutron star, energy is released — a <u>lot</u> of energy! For example, a single sweet dropped onto a neutron star would release energy equal to that of the atomic bomb that destroyed Hiroshima!

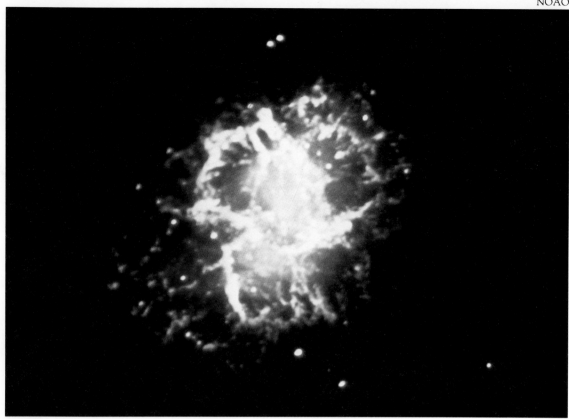

The Crab Nebula: In 1054 astronomers saw a supernova whose 'ashes' we see today as a cloud of hot gas. Today's technology can photograph the cloud to reveal its chemical parts. This photograph shows hydrogen (red) and sulfur (blue) emissions from the nebula.

Celestial Lighthouses — Neutron Stars, or Pulsars

In 1054, Chinese, Arab, and American Indian sky-watchers looked up to the heavens and saw the result of a supernova that had exploded 6,500 light-years away from us. (One light-year is how far light travels in one year.) The supernova formed a huge expanding cloud of dust and gas that we can still see. The cloud is called the Crab Nebula. At the centre is a tiny neutron star, all that is left of the exploded star. This neutron star turns 33 times a second, sending a pulse of energy toward us at each turn. This energy is in the form of electric waves called radio waves. We first noticed these pulses in the Crab Nebula in 1969 and began calling neutron stars pulsars. The Crab pulsar sends out pulses of light, too, blinking on and off 33 times a second.

Stars speaking from space!

A young astronomy student, Jocelyn Bell, first detected in 1967 the radio waves that flickered, or twinkled, rapidly from the sky. For a while, some people wondered if they were signals from beings from space. We called them LGM, for Little Green Men. But the twinkles were so regular that we decided they couldn't be of intelligent origin. Ms. Bell had discovered pulsars — spinning neutron stars sending out radio waves with each turn.

Smithsonian Institution

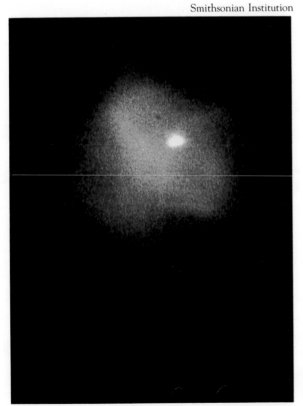

The hot inner regions of the Crab.
The bright spot is the Crab pulsar.
In one second it blinks on and off
33 times! Here it is with its light on.

A Hole in Space

We know that gravity is a force that makes objects become attracted to one another. But can you imagine what gravity actually looks like? We can picture gravity by pretending space is a rubber sheet. Any heavy object resting on the sheet puts a dent in it. The heavier the object, the deeper the dent. If an object is kept heavy but made smaller, the weight is concentrated on a smaller area, and the dent gets deeper. A white dwarf makes a much deeper dent than the Earth does, and a neutron star makes a still deeper dent. The deeper the dent, the harder it would be to get out of if you fell in. What if something is so small and heavy that it forms a dent too deep for anything to get out of — ever!

Pulsars — you can set your watch by them!

Pulsars turn so steadily that astronomers could use them as nearly perfect clocks. In fact, pulsars have even been used to chart Earth's position in the Galaxy. On board the Pioneer 10 and 11 space probes are plaques that tell about Earth. The locations of pulsars are used as maps on these plaques. Scientists knew that the rates at which these pulsars turned would change very little in the time it might take for these plaques to be discovered in space — perhaps millions of years. So these maps would help extraterrestrial beings find the location of Earth from anywhere in the Galaxy.

This diagram shows the pull of the gravitational fields of several stellar objects: from left to right, the Sun, a neutron star, and a black hole. See how the large Sun barely distorts the grid. The smaller neutron star further distorts the grid with its more concentrated mass. And the smallest object — the black hole — distorts the grid lines most of all with its tremendous gravitational pull.

Black Holes

It is hard to fight the gravity of smaller, more massive objects. A neutron star, for instance, is almost impossible to get away from. Only light, radio waves, and electrons can get away.

And if a massive object were still smaller, nothing could get away from it.

Even light couldn't get away!

If everything fell in and nothing came out, it would be like a hole in space. If even light couldn't come out, we would call it a black hole.

If a large star explodes, and if its remaining matter becomes small and tightly packed enough, it might become a black hole!

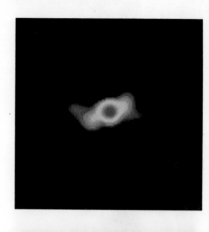
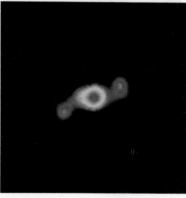

NRAO

Double pulsars — a recipe for trouble?

Astronomers have found cases where two pulsars are close and circling each other. All the while, they are giving off radiation and losing energy. This means they get slightly closer at each turn. Eventually, they will collide. What will happen when two pulsars collide? The mass will double. It might grow so large that additional gravity will cause it to collapse into a black hole. How would the formation of such a black hole appear to our instruments? We just don't know.

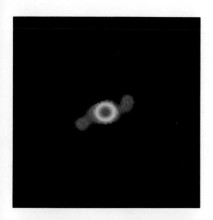

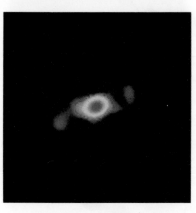

These four pictures, taken by a radio telescope, show a star called SS 433 at one-month intervals. The star is shooting out twin jets of hot gas from its center. The jets are moving away from the star at a speed of 290 million km (180 million miles) per hour — one-quarter the speed of light! Some scientists think that this star may be a black hole.

NRAO

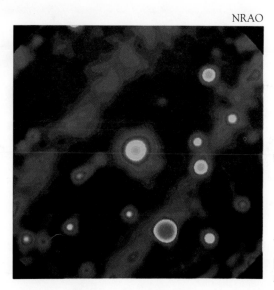

This radio image records a possible black hole in the Andromeda galaxy.

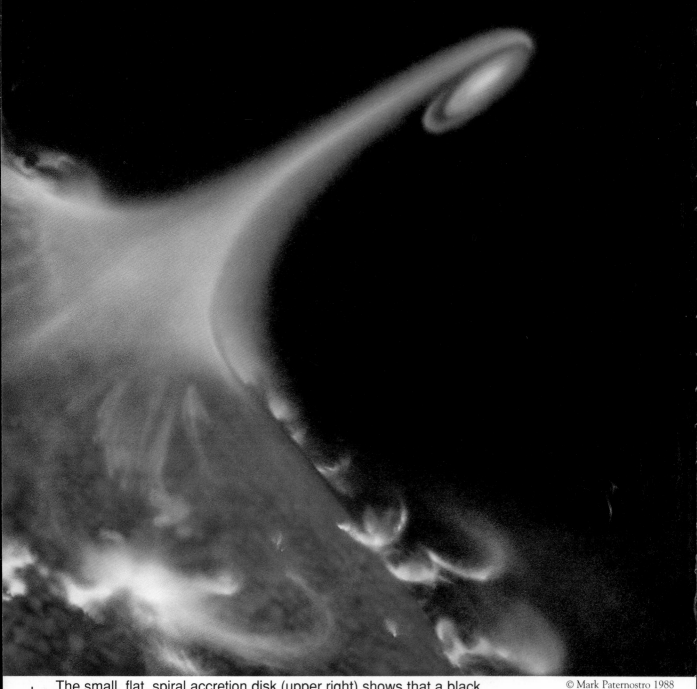

The small, flat, spiral accretion disk (upper right) shows that a black hole is stealing matter from its neighbouring star. X-rays given off by the whirling matter tell us that we are looking at a black hole. The black hole itself is invisible.

Finding Black Holes

If even light can't get out of a black hole, how can we see it and know it's there? How can we know if black holes exist?

Well, we know because of matter from nearby stars. If the black hole is near some star, it attracts matter from the star. The matter whirls around and around the black hole, creating a flat spiral called an accretion disk. As the matter whirls, it gives off x-rays, loses energy, and finally falls into the black hole. We can't see the black hole, but we can detect the x-rays. In the constellation Cygnus, for example, astronomers have detected x-rays from a large star that seems to be whirling around something we can't see.

That 'something' is probably a black hole.

Mini-black holes: a maxi-problem?

A scientist, Stephen Hawking, has shown that black holes can very slowly evaporate and turn into thin gas. The smaller they are, the more quickly they evaporate. When the Universe began, perhaps black holes of all sizes were formed. Some might have been mini-black holes, having about the same mass as planets or even asteroids. If these are scattered through space, we won't be able to detect them unless they are really close. What would happen to us if a mini-black hole approached our Solar system? We don't know. But let's hope it would evaporate before it got here!

© Mark Paternostro 1988

Astronomers think this is what the central depths of some galaxies may look like: a black hole at the centre both drawing in stellar matter and shooting out jets of excess matter that the black hole cannot absorb quickly enough. These jets shoot out way beyond the galaxy.

What's Going On in There?

We can't see into the central depths of a galaxy. A mass of stars blocks the view. Radiation in the form of radio waves and x-rays comes out of the centre, however, and we can detect that radiation. It takes a lot of energy to form that radiation. Where does it come from? Some astronomers suspect there are black holes at the centres of at least some galaxies. Matter from nearby stars spirals in, producing the radiation. Ordinary black holes, like the one in Cygnus, may only be as massive as large stars. But black holes in the centres of some galaxies may be as massive as a million stars, or even a billion stars! Think of all that mass squeezed together so tightly: The gravitational pull of these centres must be incredible!

Halton C. Arp   Smithsonian Institution

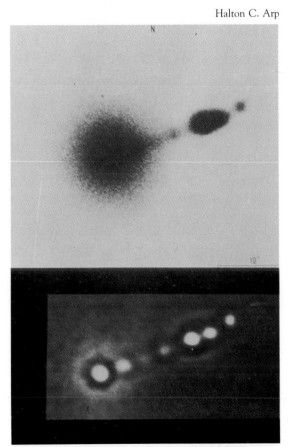 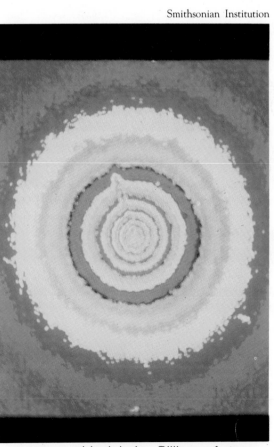

The giant elliptical galaxy called M87 seems to centre on a black hole. Billions of stars appear to orbit about a huge object that does not give off light, and scientists think that a black hole centre may have consumed the mass of five billion stars the size of our Sun! In these pictures, you can detect the jet projecting from M87's core.

Quasars — Light from the Edge of the Universe?

The Universe never stops coming up with objects to fascinate and puzzle us. One group of objects looked like faint stars. Astronomers once thought these objects were ordinary stars of our own Galaxy — except that they gave off radio waves. But then astronomers watched them closely and studied their light. In 1963, astronomers figured out that these objects were anywhere from one billion to ten billion light-years away. Astronomers soon found many more of these 'stars' that were not radio sources but were just as distant. And as recently as 1987, British and American astronomers detected an object that may be 12 billion light-years away. These objects are galaxies so far off that they wouldn't normally be seen except that their centres are unusually bright — a hundred times brighter than ordinary galactic centres. These centres are called quasars.

The word quasar comes from two words, 'quasi' and 'stellar'. Together, these two words mean 'star-like'. What makes quasars bright may be large black holes at their centres. These black holes would draw in all sorts of glowing stellar matter, from stars to dust.

NOAO

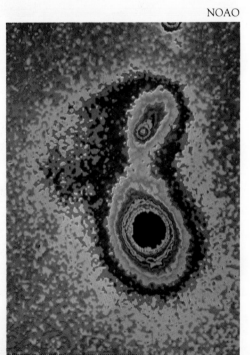

A quasar (top) interacting with a nearby galaxy and drawing in matter to the quasar's centre.

22

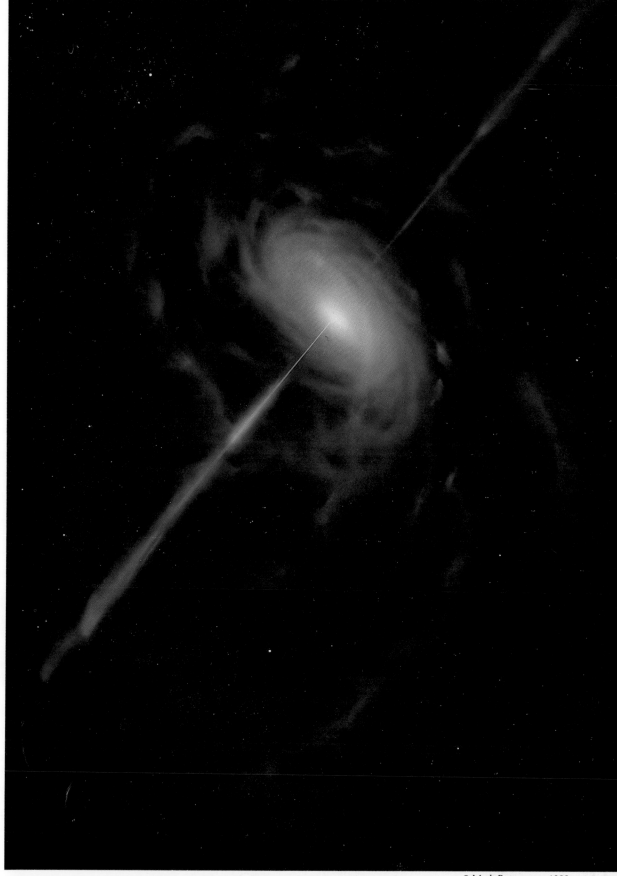

If we could see to the edge of the Universe, might we find newly-formed galaxies like this spiral with a quasar as its nucleus?

Seeing Red

How can we tell quasars are so far away? Because certain instruments can spread the light from any star into a rainbow, or a spectrum, of red, orange, yellow, green, blue, indigo, and violet. Across the rainbow are dark lines. When something that gives off light is moving away from us, the dark lines move, or shift, toward the red end of the spectrum. The faster it travels, the farther the shift toward red. Since the Universe is expanding, distant objects are all moving away and show this red shift. The greater the red shift, the farther they are!

The red shift at a glance. A galaxy's hydrogen atoms can emit blue light, as seen in the galaxy at left. However, that same light will appear redder and redder as we look at galaxies located farther from Earth, as shown by the galaxies farther to the right in this picture. The lines on the spectrum below also show a greater shift toward the red end of the spectrum as the galaxies move farther away from Earth.

When quasars were first discovered, they showed a greater red shift than anything else. That is why scientists felt that quasars were the farthest known objects in the Universe. But in 1988, astronomers from the University of Arizona, USA, announced that they had detected objects that might even be farther away — and older — than any known quasar. These objects might be as far as 17 billion light-years away! Scientists think they might be primeval galaxies. These would not be quasars. They would be galaxies in their very earliest stages of development.

NOAO

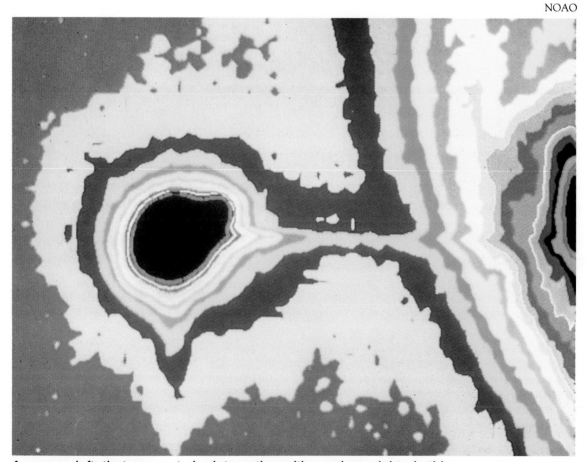

A quasar, left, that seems to be interacting with a galaxy, right. In this computer-enhanced picture, the two together resemble a chicken! The big question: Are the 'head' and the 'body' actually attached by the 'neck' of connecting material? Most astronomers believe the quasar is actually many times farther away than the galaxy.

Was the Milky Way a Quasar?

When we see a quasar 12 billion light-years away, the light from it took 12 billion years to reach us. This means we see the quasar as it was 12 billion years ago. This would be when it — and the Universe, which we think is 15-20 billion years old — were very young. So the fact that quasars are so far away may mean that young galaxies, which shine very brightly, are more likely to be quasars than old ones are. Perhaps our own Milky Way Galaxy was a quasar billions of years ago, but then it settled down. If so, that's a good thing. A galactic centre burning away as brightly as a quasar does would fill the Galaxy with so much energy that it might be impossible for life to develop in it. And without life in our Galaxy, we would not be here today!

NRAO

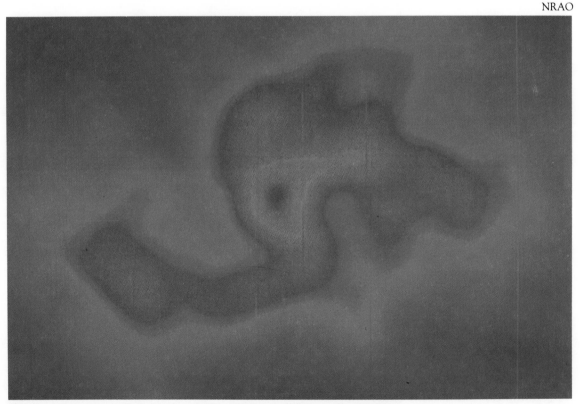

The centre of our Galaxy, the Milky Way, emitting radio waves produced by hot gas. In this false-colour picture the red shows where the gas is most dense. Could we be just 30,000 light-years away from a black hole?

The Milky Way and Andromeda galaxies: Will they collide? Or will they just slide past each other, sending our Sun spinning off for good? Whatever happens, we've got four billion years to make other plans.

Close encounters of the galactic kind — a major crack-up in our future?

Our Milky Way and the Andromeda galaxy are moving about in the same cluster. Sometimes we are farther apart, and sometimes we are closer together. Recently a scientist found evidence that the two galaxies will collide in about four billion years. Imagine these two colossal star systems — each containing hundreds of billions of stars — smacking into each other! In fact, though, there is lots of room between the stars in each galaxy and few, if any, stars would actually collide. The galaxies would just slide through each other! But the galaxies would be shaken by gravity, and our own Sun could go spinning off, leaving its home galaxy forever. But don't worry just yet — four billion years is a long time from now!

© Michael Carroll 1987

A

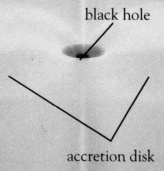

gas jet

black hole

accretion disk

B

Fact File: Quasars and Black Holes

Quasars. What we can see of them comes to us from distances so vast that we can barely imagine how far away — and how long ago — they existed. Some are believed to be 12 billion light-years away, and for years astronomers thought they were the oldest visible objects in the Universe. Astronomers now believe they have spotted objects that could be as distant as 17 billion light-years away. These are primeval galaxies. We see them as they were in the earliest stages of their creation, before the Universe was old enough to spawn quasars. But quasars still win the prize for power, since most astronomers still believe that they are the most powerful energy sources in the sky.

On the opposite page are two pictures. Picture A is of a spiral galaxy with a quasar at its core. Picture B gives us a close-up of the core, showing the black hole that may lie at the heart of a quasar.

Picture A:

Subject:
- A violent spiral galaxy deep in the cosmos.

Special features:
- High-energy quasar at galactic core.
- Possible black hole at centre.
- Accretion disk — a gravitational whirlpool of hot gas in a ring around the centre feeding the black hole and the quasar.
- Gas jets spewing excess particles at right angles to disk.

Picture B:

Subject:
- A detailed view of the galactic core, showing the quasar and its black hole centre.

Special features:
- Sideways view of accretion disk. The disk might stretch out to a diameter 100 times that of our Solar system.
- Black hole at centre of disk. Because of huge amount of stellar matter swirling around the centre, the black hole would not normally be visible. A black hole like this might have the mass of billions of stars the size of our Sun crammed into a space no bigger than that of our Solar system.
- Jets shooting matter at a right angle to the accretion disk. This is matter that is in excess of what the black hole can absorb. The matter shoots out to distances that could approach millions of light-years. This would be farther than the distance between our Milky Way and its nearest galactic neighbour, the Andromeda galaxy.

More Books About Quasars, Pulsars, and Black Holes

Here are more books about quasars, pulsars, black holes, and other stellar objects. If you are interested in them, check your library or bookshop.

Black Holes, Quasars and Other Mysteries of the Universe Gibilisco (Tab Books, US)
Black Holes, Quasars and the Universe. Shipman (Houghton Mifflin)
How We Found Out About Black Holes. Asimov (Longman)
Our Milky Way and Other Galaxies. Asimov (Gareth Stevens)
Picture Library Series: Satellites. Barrett (Franklin Watts)
Stars. Couper (Franklin Watts)

Places to Visit

You can explore quasars, pulsars, black holes, and other unusual things in the Universe without leaving Earth. Here are some museums and centres where you can find a variety of space exhibits.

The Science Museum
London

The Royal Observatory
Edinburgh, Scotland

The Exploratorium
Bristol, Avon

Armagh Planetarium
Armagh, Northern Ireland

The Royal Greenwich Observatory
Herstmonceux Castle, Hailsham, Sussex

The London Planetarium
London

For More Information About Quasars, Pulsars, and Black Holes

Here are some places you can write to for more information about quasars, pulsars and black holes. Be sure to tell them exactly what you want to know about or see. Remember to include your age, full name and address so they can write back to you.

For photography of stars and galaxies:
Science Museum Library
Photo Orders Service
South Kensington
London   SW7 5HN

For information about astronomy:
European Space Agency
Public Relations Department
810 Rue Mario Nikis
75738 Paris 15

For catalogues of slides, posters and other astronomy material:
Earth and Sky
21A West End
Hebden Bridge
West Yorkshire
HX7 8UQ

Spaceprints
17A High Street
Norton
Stockton-on-Tees
Cleveland

Glossary

accretion disk: a ring of interstellar matter surrounding a star or other object, such as a black hole, which has an intense gravitational field.

Bell, Jocelyn: the British astronomer who first detected what later were known as pulsars.

billion: In the United States, the number represented by 1 followed by nine zeroes — 1,000,000,000. In other countries, such as Britain, this number is called 'a thousand million'. In these countries, one billion would then be represented by 1 followed by *12* zeroes — 1,000,000,000,000: a million million, which is called a 'trillion' in this book.

black hole: a massive object — usually a collapsed star — so tightly packed that not even light can escape the force of its gravity.

Crab Nebula: a huge expanding cloud of dust and gas that is visible from Earth. It was first reported in 1054 and is the result of a supernova.

galaxy: any of the many large groupings of stars, gas, and dust that exist in the Universe. Our galaxy is known as the Milky Way.

Hawking, Stephen: the Cambridge mathematician and physicist who has shown that black holes can slowly evaporate and turn into thin gas.

helium: a light, colourless gas that makes up part of every star.

hydrogen: a colourless, odorless gas that is the simplest and lightest of the elements. Stars are three-quarters hydrogen.

Milky Way: the name of our Galaxy.

neutron star: a star with all the mass of an ordinary large star that has had its mass squeezed into a small ball.

one light-year: the distance that light travels in one year — nearly 9.5 trillion km, or six trillion miles.

Orion Nebula: one of the huge clouds of dust and gas in which stars are forming.

pulsar: a neutron star sending out rapid pulses of light or electrical waves.

quasar: a 'star-like' core of a galaxy that may have a large black hole at its centre.

red giants: huge stars that develop when their hydrogen runs low and the extra heat makes them expand. Their outer layers then change to a cool red.

Solar system: the Sun, planets and all other bodies that orbit the Sun.

supernova: a red giant that has collapsed, heating its cool outer layers and causing explosions.

Universe: everything we know that exists and believe may exist.

white dwarf: the small, white-hot body that remains when a star like our Sun collapses.

Index

The publishers wish to thank the following for permission to reproduce copyright material: front cover, pp. 4-5 (upper), 8, 9 (lower), 18, 20, 23, 28 (lower), © Mark Paternostro 1988; p. 27, © Mark Paternostro 1983; pp. 5 (lower), 12, 22, 25, National Optical Astronomy Observatories; pp. 6-7, © Sally Bensusen 1987; p. 9 (upper), European Space Agency; p. 15, © Julian Baum 1988; pp. 10-11 (upper), © Lynette Cook 1988; pp. 10-11 (lower), courtesy of William Priedhorsky, Los Alamos National Laboratory; pp. 13, 21 (right), Smithsonian Institution; pp. 16-17 (all), 26, National Radio Astronomy Observatory; p. 21 (two at left), courtesy of Halton C. Arp; p. 24, © Adolf Schaller 1988; p. 28 (upper), © Michael Carroll 1987.